Research It!

Medieval Europe

Stewart Ross

Heinemann Library
Chicago, Illinois

www.heinemannraintree.com
Visit our website to find out more information about Heinemann-Raintree books.

To order:
☎ Phone 888-454-2279
💻 Visit www.heinemannraintree.com to browse our catalog and order online.

Edited by Andrew Farrow
Designed by Steven Mead
Map on p. 12 by David Woodroffe,
 © Capstone Global Library Ltd
Picture research by Ruth Blair
Production by Victoria Fitzgerald
Originated by Capstone Global Library Ltd
Printed and bound in China by South China Printing Company Ltd

14 13 12 11 10
10 9 8 7 6 5 4 3 2 1

Library of Congress Cataloging-in-Publication Data
Ross, Stewart.
  Medieval Europe / Stewart Ross.
    p. cm. -- (Research it!)
  ISBN 978-1-4329-3498-9 (hc)
  1. Civilization, Medieval--Juvenile literature.
2. Europe--Civilization--Juvenile literature. 3. Europe--History--476-1492--Juvenile literature.
I. Title.
  CB351.R585 2009
  940.1--dc22
                    2009008760

Acknowledgments
The author and publishers are grateful to the following for permission to reproduce copyright material: Alamy: pp. **38** (©Holmes Garden Photos), **16** (©Mary Evans Picture Library); ©The Art Archive: pp. **4** (British Library), **41** (Jarrold Publishing), **48** (Museo di Capodimonte, Naples/Alfredo Dagli Orti), **35** (National Gallery Budapest/Alfredo Dagli Orti), **17** (University Library Prague/Gianni Dagli Orti); Bridgeman Art Library: p. **7** (Brabant School, 15th century/Bibliotheque de L'Arsenal, Paris, France/Archives Charmet); Corbis: p. **43** (Bryan Pickering, Eye Ubiquitous); Getty Images: pp. **44** (Ilan Arad), **28** (Hulton Archive); Mary Evans Picture Library: pp. **32** (AISA Media), **23**; Photolibrary: pp. **39** (F1 online), **37** (Photononstop); Rex Features: pp. **18** (Alinari), **31**; ©shutterstock and ©iStockphoto: background images and design features.

The main cover image of Avignon Palace in France is reproduced with permission of iStockphoto/©Fanelle Rosier. The background images are reproduced with the permission of the following: ©iStockphoto (©Olena Druzhynina, ©Dusko Jovic, ©Martin McCarthy, ©Barbara Miller) and ©shutterstock (©dpaint, ©Lars Lindblad, ©p_a_p_a, ©Picsfive, ©Craig Wactor).

We would like to thank Rebecca Vickers for her invaluable help in the preparation of this book.

Every effort has been made to contact copyright holders of material reproduced in this book. Any omissions will be rectified in subsequent printings if notice is given to the publisher.

All the Internet addresses (URLs) given in this book were valid at the time of going to press. However, due to the dynamic nature of the Internet, some addresses may have changed, or sites may have changed or ceased to exist since publication. While the author and publisher regret any inconvenience this may cause readers, no responsibility for any such changes can be accepted by either the author or the publisher.

Contents

Some words are printed in bold, **like this**. You can find out what they mean by looking in the glossary.

Why Research Medieval Europe?

"Research" means careful investigation into a subject, which is more than simply looking up information about it. But scholars have been researching medieval Europe for centuries: What is the point of doing further independent research if all the facts are already known?

This misunderstands what history is. History is the study of past events—all past events. Each individual has a personal history, which is the story of his or her life. So, in theory the history of the reign of Frederick I of Germany (Frederick "Barbarossa," 1152–90) is the sum of the histories—every second of every minute of every hour—of the hundreds of thousands of people with whom he was involved. That is billions of tiny pieces of information, more than any one historian could ever hope to master.

England's King Richard II (who ruled 1377–99) meets Anne of Bohemia for an arranged marriage in 1382. Sources like this are open equally to interpretation by all historians, professional and amateur.

The historical process

What historians do, therefore, is select what seems to be the most important information, interpret it, and **generalize** about it:

Select → Interpret → Generalize

So, when researching you must remember that:

- All the facts will never be known.
- Each researcher makes his or her own selection, **interpretation**, and generalization.

The outcomes of historical research will always vary, because no two people view the past in the same way. The process and its results depend on variables such as the position of the researchers—issues such as their **gender**, age, nationality, and upbringing—and the date at which the research is done.

Using KWL

Researching a huge subject area like medieval Europe, which was a quite long historical period and covered a wide geographical area, can be very difficult. One way to approach it

What can affect research?

- The position of the researcher: One example in which the position of the researcher could affect the way an historical event is seen is the **Crusades**. This was an attempt by medieval Christian armies from Western Europe to take control of the **Holy Lands** of the Middle East from the Muslims. A **devout** Muslim student would almost certainly view these wars very differently from a Christian one, or from someone with no particular religious standpoint.
- The date of the research: Opinions about what is important or relevant to research change with time. A modern scholar researching the monarchs of medieval Europe would place far more emphasis on the roles played by queens and other women than a scholar who looked at the same topic a century ago.

can be to use the **KWL** method—What I **K**now, What I **W**ant to know, What I have **L**earned. In the chart below, this method has been used to summarize what has been discussed so far about researching medieval Europe.

What I **K**now	What I **W**ant to know	What I have **L**earned
There is a huge amount of research information available on medieval Europe.	Why should I do more research? Can't I just read a book or visit a website written by someone else?	History is about selection, interpretation, and generalization. These strategies change over time and with the background of each researcher. My research findings will be as valid and original as anyone's.

What exactly is research?

Research is really a quest for **evidence**. Like detectives, historians work with evidence. This is information about the past that they gather when doing research. Generally speaking, evidence can be divided in two types:

1. Written evidence, usually known as a **source**.
2. Visual, audible, or **tangible** evidence. Visual and audible evidence are usually recognized as sources, but tangible evidence, such as a castle or a battlefield, is normally not.

Evaluating sources

To evaluate the usefulness of a piece of evidence, you can use the **5 Ws** test:

- <u>Who</u> produced the evidence? Were they informed on the subject you want to know about?
- <u>What</u> exactly is the evidence? For instance, is it original or the copy of an original? If a copy, what sort is it?
- <u>When</u> was it produced? For example, a monk writing 100 years later about the number of people who fought in a battle would probably be a less reliable source of information than a copy of the soldiers' payments from the time.
- <u>Where</u> was it produced? Obviously, a French account of the Battle of Agincourt (an English victory in 1415, in the 100 Years' War) would differ from one written in England.
- <u>Why</u> was it produced? Was the author of a document trying to tell the **objective** truth, or was he or she making a political or religious point?

Handling evidence

The four stages in handling evidence are generally:

1. Find the evidence
2. **Evaluate** the evidence
3. Organize the evidence
4. Present the evidence.

This book will take you through those stages. A useful tool for handling written evidence, which you will encounter later as well, is **SQ3R**:

- *Survey* the **document** to decide whether or not it will be of use.
- *Question*—What questions will the document answer?
- *Read* the document, taking notes.

This image shows a 15th-century illustration of an 11th-century battle between Crusaders and Turks. Because of the hundreds of years between the event and the image, historians must be very careful when using pictures such as this for research.

- *Recall* the key points of the document. Do they tie in with other research?
- *Review* by re-reading the document, checking your notes, and perhaps discussing what you have found with someone else.

Historical objectivity

History, ultimately, is the search for truth. This is especially difficult when studying religious topics or those where two nations come into conflict. For example, during the early medieval period, there was conflict over whether Portugal was an independent kingdom or part of neighboring León and Castile in Spain. So, both Portuguese and Spanish students have to be careful not to let national feeling color their search for the truth on this topic.

A note on language

Language is a major difficulty for students of this period. Most documents are incomprehensible to many students, for three reasons. First, they were handwritten in styles that we find difficult to read. (Printing appeared in Europe only in the late 15th century.) Second, many documents, especially formal and church ones, were written in medieval **Latin**. Third, even those documents written in the **vernacular** (everyday local language) are difficult to read because medieval language was very different from modern languages.

Here is an example that uses words that are almost modern—the opening of a letter from Agnes Paston to her son John, written in about 1444:

> Son, I greet you well, and let you weet [know], that forasmuch [since] as your brother Clement letteth me weet that ye desire faithfully my blessing . . .
>
> (from John Fenn and Mrs. Archer-Hind, *The Paston Letters*, 2 vol., New York: Dutton, 1956)

Remember, therefore, that most documents you handle, unless they are photocopies of originals, will already have been edited and perhaps translated. They will be not quite original.

Eight steps to a well-researched paper, topic, or essay

To produce a worthwhile presentation or report based on sound research, it can be useful to follow the eight steps described in this book, which are listed below:

Step 1—The overview. Look at why medieval Europe is an important area to study, examine the geographical background, and create a timeline of major events.

Step 2—Researching the basic facts. Discover the facts that all historians agree are essential to a broad understanding of medieval Europe—and where to find them.

Step 3—Choosing and researching a topic: Learn how to find and use books and websites that provide more detailed information on aspects of medieval Europe.

Step 4—Documents: Learn about the range of documents available from the period we are studying, and how to use them in research.

Step 5—Images: Some of the most exciting evidence from medieval Europe is in the form of art. How can a researcher use it?

Step 6—Other evidence: From landscapes to armor, houses to cathedrals, what is the researcher to make of these rich sources of evidence?

Step 7—Developing your viewpoint: Examine how and why historians use research evidence to reach conclusions about the past.

Step 8—Presentation: Learn a few tips on writing and checking a sound historical paper or oral presentation.

Primary and secondary sources

Historians often distinguish between primary sources and secondary sources.

Primary sources
Primary sources date from the time under examination. In other words, they are part of the fabric of that period. They include things like **chronicles**, letters, financial documents, laws, **charters**, and even artwork, poems, and plays. An example of a primary source is a chronicle, in old French, of the Fourth Crusade (1199–1204) by Robert de Cléry: *La Conquête de Constantinople* (*The Conquest of Constantinople*).

Some primary sources are more useful than others. When consulting them, use the 5 Ws test. This example is based on Geoffrey Chaucer's famous work of fiction, the *Canterbury Tales*:

Who: Chaucer was a civil servant, MP, **courtier**, and poet who lived c. 1340–1400.
What: Chaucer's fictional masterpiece, the *Canterbury Tales*, is a series of stories supposedly told by **pilgrims** as they travel to the shrine of St. Thomas in Canterbury.
When: The *Canterbury Tales* was written in the 1390s.
Where: Chaucer traveled widely around western Europe, finally retiring to Kent, England, where he wrote the *Tales*.
Why: The *Tales* were written to entertain and, in places, criticize English society in Chaucer's day.

Asking the 5 Ws puts you in a good position to ask yourself how useful the *Canterbury Tales* is as a primary source of information on medieval Europe (see also p. 35).

Secondary sources
Secondary sources are accounts or interpretations of events written by historians, journalists, and others. Some, especially if they are the product of years of research using primary sources, are especially valuable and reliable.

Researchers use both primary and secondary sources. Ideally, your research into medieval Europe should try to do the same.

Step 1: Overview

The topic of medieval Europe is absolutely enormous! Within it are all the events in an entire continent over 500 years. That is more than any person can ever hope to get a grasp of in much detail.

If you feel your general knowledge on this topic is not very strong, take time to read the timeline (pp. 14–15) and then, before you go any further, read the glossary at the end of the book (pp. 52–53). During your research, remember that for most of the medieval period, it is unwise to speak of "countries" other than as geographical expressions. Germany, Spain, and Italy, for example, were simply regions divided into many small states. Wales was amalgamated with England only in the late 13th century, and Scotland was an independent kingdom until 1707. To keep your research under control and clear in your mind, always refer back to the KWL tool:

- What I **K**now
- What I **W**ant to Know
- What I Have **L**earned.

We also need to understand exactly what the word "medieval" means. It is the adjective used for the term "Middle Ages" to describe the 1,100 years (400–1500 CE) between "ancient" history and "modern" history— between the collapse of the Roman Empire and the beginning of the European **Renaissance**.

During the centuries immediately following the collapse of the Roman Empire, Europe was a seriously troubled region. It was frequently invaded, law and order suffered, learning and scholarship fell to a low level, and there was political instability. Historians used to speak of the years 400–800 CE as the "Dark Ages" because so little written evidence from that period survives.

This book focuses largely on the relatively settled years 1000–1500 CE. The principal features of this period were:

- Growth of law and ordered government
- Expansion of towns, **commerce**, and trade
- **Gothic** art and architecture
- The Roman Catholic Church, based on **monasteries**, which covered all of Europe (known as "**Christendom**")
- The Crusades.

Aspects of any of these areas are excellent research topics.

The physical context

Geography provides the stage on which the drama of history is played out. We need to know two things about the geography of medieval Europe:

1. The physical features that influenced the way the continent developed and the way its rulers behaved. The Alps, for instance, formed a major barrier between the Italian peninsula and the rest of the continent.
2. The shifting political borders. Medieval Europe was a patchwork of small states, some only a single city. Other borders, such as the boundaries of **bishoprics** and of the **Holy Roman Empire**, were also important.

Research using maps

To get a handle on the medieval geography of Europe, maps are the most useful research tool. It is important to have an idea before you start of what you are looking for. "What medieval Europe looked like" is too vague, so:

- limit your research to a specific topic
- make a list of the specific maps you require. Using a KWL chart will help.

For example, if you are researching the Crusades, remember that history is about change, and that the Crusades took place over hundreds of years. The physical shape of Europe did not alter over that period, but plenty of boundaries did. One single map, therefore, will probably not be enough.

You can use a diagram, like a triangle on its point, to narrow the number of maps you need. This example shows how to use this method to get from general maps of Europe to one on a specific battle during the Third Crusade.

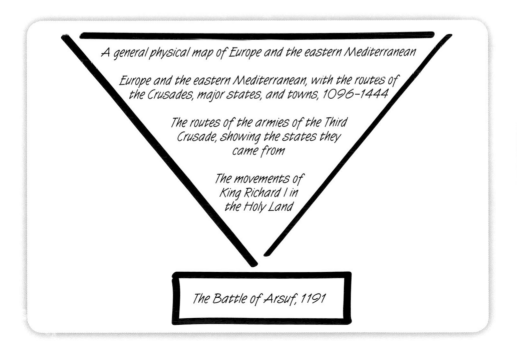

A general physical map of Europe and the eastern Mediterranean

Europe and the eastern Mediterranean, with the routes of the Crusades, major states, and towns, 1096–1444

The routes of the armies of the Third Crusade, showing the states they came from

The movements of King Richard I in the Holy Land

The Battle of Arsuf, 1191

Where to look for maps

Here are four possible sources to use when looking for information from maps:

- General atlases—*Advantages*: These are fine for understanding the physical geography of Europe, such as mountains and deserts. A good physical features map, for example, is needed to understand how the Crusaders reached the Holy Land.

  Disadvantages: These are bad for political information, especially boundaries. For example, a modern map will show Germany as a single country, whereas medieval Germany was composed of many political and religious states and other groupings. Berlin is not even mentioned before 1244, and many place names have changed (see below).

- Internet—*Advantages*: The Internet has some useful historical maps, but it is hard to locate and evaluate them. Google Earth is an exciting way of zeroing in on a physical feature. In order to help understand why King Richard did not attempt to attack Jerusalem, go to "Jerusalem" on a map and examine the surrounding landscape.

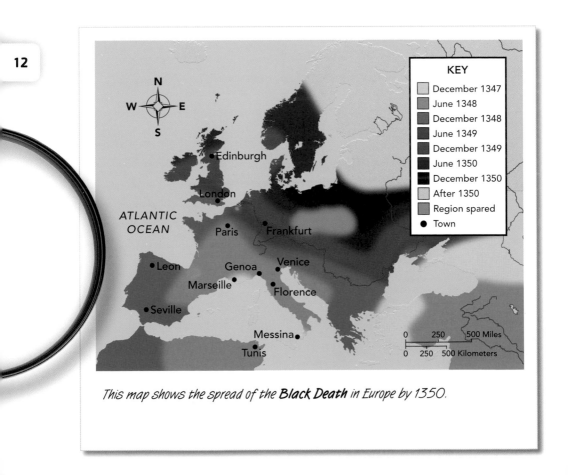

This map shows the spread of the Black Death in Europe by 1350.

Disadvantages: Most political and historical maps available for free on the Internet are short on detail and often unreliable. Also it is difficult to find what you want in one place. Physical geography maps on the Internet are notoriously poor in quality. For maps relating to medieval Europe, therefore, this is not a good place to start.

- Books—*Advantages*: Maps are usually reliable. They are better for specific places (the Battle of Arsuf of 1191, for example) rather than the bigger picture because they are often too small.
Disadvantages: Maps are there to support the text, so they may not contain the information you want.
- Historical atlases—*Advantages*: They have just what you need—maps produced by historians for historians, checked for accuracy and covering every angle you could wish for.
Disadvantages: You may find an historical atlas so fascinating that you waste time browsing through the whole thing.

Making research notes on maps

Taking notes from maps is not easy. Don't just trace the maps or make photocopies or printouts—make your own rough sketch-map versions of them as well. This means you will have to look carefully at the information in the maps and digest and understand what they show.

Problems with place names

There are three significant problems with place names when researching medieval Europe:

- Place names vary: A good example is **Constantinople**, now Istanbul, the old capital city of the Eastern Roman Empire. It was also known as **Byzantium**.
- Place names have changed: Names that were used in the Middle Ages—such as Bohemia (the Czech Republic), Alba (Scotland), and the Papal States (in central Italy)—are now hardly used or have disappeared altogether.
- Place names differ from language to language: Some changes are minor, such as the English "Florence" being "Firenze" in modern Italian and "Fiorenza" in old Italian. A far trickier example is the German town of Aachen, known as "Oche" in Dutch, "Aquisgrán" in Italian, "Aquisgrana" in French, and "Aix-la-Chapelle" in English!

Step 2: Researching the Basic Facts

Historical research is seeking information. This is not necessarily just specific facts, like names and dates, but also interpretations and opinions. "Interpretation" means understanding the significance of a fact. For example, how did the 1358 Peasants' Revolt in France relate to that country's setbacks in the 100 Years' War? Some historians have argued their interpretation like this: After the capture of France's King John II by the English in 1356,

- the French government collapsed
- landowners took advantage of the chaos to increase taxes
- peasant fury exploded into rebellion against their social superiors.

Other historians trace the original causes of the revolt back to long-term food shortages.

Opinion is more personal. For example, an historian influenced by the ideas of the German political and economic philosopher Karl Marx (the 19th-century father of modern communism) might see the Peasants' Revolt as part of the changes from a **feudal** to a capitalist society.

Here England's King Richard II is shown meeting peasant rebels in 1371. Over the years, historians have interpreted the famous Peasants' Revolt in a number of different ways.

Starting your research

There are all sorts of places to start a quest for basic information about medieval Europe: different types of books, the Internet, documentary movies, and discussion with experts.

Documentary movies
Advantages: They are easy to access, usually lively, and entertaining; many contain primary evidence, and they can be visually memorable.
Disadvantages: They are limited in what they cover and often focus on aspects that look good on screen, such as cathedrals and castles. They are made to provide entertainment and make money, and there is no guarantee they are objective. They are unlikely to be the best starting point for research.

Talking to an expert
Advantages: It is interesting, you are able to ask for explanation and/or repetition of points that are not clear, and you can ask the specific questions you want answered.
Disadvantages: It may be hard to find an expert—and how do you know that someone calling himself or herself an expert really is one? This is unlikely to be the best way to start your research.

Internet web searches
Advantages: It is quick and easy and there are a lot of options.
Disadvantages: The vast quantities of information (for example, you get 12 million hits for "medieval Europe" on Google!), and the fact that it is hard to distinguish a valid, accurate site from an invalid one. There is no absolute way to judge a site's objectivity, accuracy, or thoroughness. So, a general web search is exciting and fun, but it is rarely the best way to begin researching a topic, especially one as broad as medieval Europe.

This picture shows blood-letting, a common practice in medieval medicine for treating illnesses. Only some sources will give you useful and accurate information about this subject.

Using the Internet

More information is available to an online student than anything contained in the largest school library ever built. Many resources can be found using online research **databases** or through websites accessed via search engines. The strengths of using a search engine are also its weaknesses, as it will simply find websites linked to the word or words you entered, possibly millions of choices. Most schools have access to some databases. Research databases are usually developed, and their information selected and checked for accuracy, for a specific audience, such as students of a particular grade level. As online research databases are usually subscription services (where membership or payment is required), school and public libraries join on behalf of their users. Ask your teacher or a librarian what is available and for a user name and password.

This section of the famous Bayeux Tapestry depicts Norman horsemen attacking English foot soldiers at the Battle of Hastings in 1066. The Internet and research databases can be rich resources for viewing images you cannot see locally.

Stages in website research
Choose your topic: general information on medieval Europe.
1. Decide which words to enter into the "search" box. The first word often carries the most weight. So, "medieval Europe," "Europe medieval," "middle ages Europe," and "Europe middle ages" might all produce different site lists.
2. Do an advanced search. For example, Google lets you eliminate unhelpful words and choose pages only in English.
3. Glance through the listed sites. The 3Rs method offers ways to judge usefulness at this stage in the process. First **R**: Is the site relevant? Is the site really about medieval Europe? It could be a link to information about a band called "Medieval Europe." Second **R**: Is the site reliable? Can you trust the site? By and large, two groups of sites are the most reliable. Those created by a public organization or an institution with a good **academic** reputation, such as a university (often with a web

address that contains .edu), are usually okay. Commercial **subscription sites** that you need to pay to use, such as *Encyclopedia Britannica*, usually have their facts checked for accuracy. Do not trust personal sites or blogs set up by enthusiastic amateurs. Their attractive simplicity is often the result of ignorance. Third R: Is it the right level? Is the site designed for someone at your grade level? Read some of the

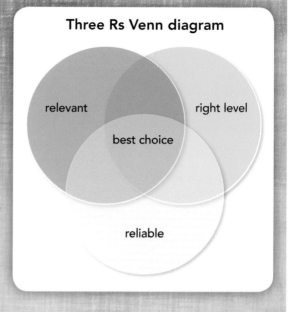

Three Rs Venn diagram

relevant

right level

best choice

reliable

text carefully before judging. Finding a site that looks helpful and then pressing "print" simply wastes paper.

4. Jot down the titles, or URLs, of the four most useful sites. Remember, the order in which they appear on the search engine page reflects their popularity and relevance to the search words, not their usefulness to you. Go through several pages of lists before choosing.

5. Take notes from the chosen sites. This is essential—you learn nothing by printing out and filing, or cutting and pasting! (See page 26.) Notes can be taken directly from the screen or from printed text. Again, the SQ3R tool may come in handy: Survey the site, note any questions that arise, read the site carefully taking notes as you go, recall key facts, and review what you have achieved.

You can also use the 5 Ws as a tool to judge Internet sites:

• Who created the site?

• What precisely is the site? Is it a course outline, a **bibliography** (see page 22), or an information site? Is it a translation?

• When was the site produced? It might be out of date in some of its interpretations.

• Where was the site produced? Is a site on medieval Europe created in Ireland likely to be more reliable than one created in Mongolia?

• Why was the site produced? Should you trust a site created by a student (even with an .edu address) to display his or her own research work?

Research using books

Books are the traditional, tried and tested way of passing on information. Like Internet sites, however, they must be approached with caution.

Advantages: There are books written specifically for students, which are easy to take notes from, likely to be accurate, and easy to use.

Disadvantages: There are so many books that it is not easy to decide which ones are the most appropriate. If you have to buy them, nonfiction books can be expensive.

Books are business

The key point about books (and subscription Internet sites) is that they are created by businesses—success or failure depends on whether customers buy their products. Students, schools, and colleges will buy a specific book only if it is:

- relevant
- at the appropriate level
- accessible
- accurate.

Authors and publishers *have* to get their books right—or they go out of business. For that reason, an appropriate book is almost certainly going to be the best place to start your research.

What book?

So, which type of book makes the best starting point for research into medieval Europe? There are two choices: information books and encyclopedias. Most of the good books covering all of medieval Europe are written for adults and are so long that you could spend all your research time taking notes from just one volume.

A general or historical encyclopedia aimed at researchers your age is a much better bet. The advantages of this type of encyclopedia are that it will:

- be written at the appropriate level
- be brief
- be accurate
- have good links to further information (**footnote** and bibliography entries).

Selecting encyclopedias

Encyclopedias come in all sorts, shapes, and sizes, ranging from the massive adult version of the *Encyclopedia Britannica* to CD and online versions of encyclopedias specifically for young people. Many adult encyclopedias have school or student editions. Make sure you select the encyclopedia that is best suited to your level.

For example, in the *World Book* encyclopedia, the medieval Europe article is entitled "Middle Ages." It is written by a professor from a respected university and runs to just over 5,000 words, making it ideal as a first research read. Once you have chosen the article or book that best suits your needs, use the SQ3R technique (Survey, Question, Read, Recall, Review) to take notes from it.

Using a bibliography

Strictly speaking, a bibliography is a list of books. It generally refers to books consulted when producing a piece of work, although the word is sometimes used more generally to mean a recommended reading list. When it includes a variety of sources, such as movies and websites, it is generally known as a list of sources.

Bibliographies, reading lists, and lists of sources can be very useful in finding material for research. They are usually placed at the end of a book or article. Most lists distinguish between primary and secondary sources, and some separate works for students from those for the general reader.

Bibliography formats

In a bibliography or source list, books are usually set out like this:
Author's last name, author's first name or initials. Title of Book. *Place of publication: publisher, date of publication.*

Websites are usually written like this:
Author's last name, author's first name or initials [if available]. "Title of Article." Title of Website. Web address (date accessed).

There are also specific styles for other sources, such as newspaper and magazine articles and encyclopedia entries. Your teacher or school may have rules about the style they prefer you to use for your bibliography, so ask before you start your research to make sure you write down all the information you need.

Taking and organizing notes

Taking notes has four functions:
1. Notes give you a neat summary of facts and ideas.
2. Notes enable you to organize information quickly and easily.
3. Taking notes makes you read a text carefully and understand it. It requires you to think about what you are reading—you cannot take sensible notes about something you don't understand.
4. Note taking helps you remember information, because ideas are processed by your brain as you write them down. This does not happen when you just read or cut and paste information.

When taking notes:
- Read the full text carefully.
- If the book or research materials are yours, mark keywords and phrases (using underlining or highlighting).
- Write down your marked words as briefly as possible using abbreviations (such as "gov" for "govern"), simple words, numbers, bullet points, underlining, headings, lots of paragraphs breaks, and colors.
- Read your notes before moving on to make sure they make sense.

Here is an example of a section of text from the *World Book* website on the relationship between a Norman king and his **barons** and the underlining you could use and type of notes that could be made from it:

From the <u>Norman</u> invasion of <u>England</u> in <u>1066</u> <u>through</u> the <u>1100s</u>, <u>most</u> of the <u>kings</u> who ruled England were <u>able and strong</u>. They usually <u>tried</u> to <u>govern justly</u> and <u>respected</u> feudal <u>law</u>. Under feudal law, <u>nobles called barons received land in return for military and other services</u> to the king. <u>Law and custom</u> established the <u>barons' duties</u> and what was <u>expected of the king</u>. But there was <u>no actual control over the king's power</u>.

Norman kings and barons, 1066-1100s
(i) Most Ks of Eng able & strong
(ii) Tried to gov justly & obey feudal law
(iii) Feud law said barons got land in return for military & other service
(iv) Law & custom set out (a) barons' duties (b) what expected of king
(v) BUT no actual limit on k's power

Footnotes and endnotes

In some books and articles, the author gives the source of a piece of information—usually a quotation—as soon as it appears. This is done by putting a small, usually raised, number immediately after the words they **cite**. The number is repeated at the bottom of the page, and next to it the source, or footnote, is given. This way, the reader knows precisely where the author found his or her information, allowing others to check it for themselves. It also helps prevent researchers from using other people's work as their own. Sometimes, instead of having a **citation** for information used at the bottom of the page, all of the citations are gathered together in a list at the end of the work. This list is usually referred to as endnotes.

This is an artist's impression of a scene from Black Death-stricken Norway in 1349. Because it was so widespread, the Black Death can provide excellent opportunities for studying the effects on specific local areas.

Step 3: Choosing and Researching a Topic

Unless you have been assigned a topic by your teacher, you will have to make the choice yourself from what is a very big subject area.

When you are choosing an assignment topic, ask yourself:

- Am I *really* interested in this topic?
- Is there plenty of material?
- Is it the right amount of information? An essay on medieval trade would be tricky because there is too much information, while there would be too little on, say, the wine trade in medieval Paris.
- Is the topic original? It is more interesting to select a topic that has not been done many times before. For example, it is better to write interestingly and in detail about a single building rather than on castles in general.

If in doubt about how to limit your topic, ask someone who will be able to help—a librarian or teacher.

Zooming in on one topic

The Black Death in England in the mid-14th century would be a good topic. Using a KWL chart would be a starting point.

What I **K**now	What I **W**ant to know	What I have **L**earned
The Black Death reached Europe in 1347. It hit England a year later and killed perhaps 50% of the population.	What social, economic, and political effects did this massive death rate have?	Nothing yet—to be completed later.

The next move is to check the usefulness, reliability, and appropriateness of the secondary sources you find. Here is an example review of a few print and Internet sources:

Source	Usefulness	Reliability	Appropriateness
Philip Ziegler. *The Black Death.* New York: Harper Perennial, 2009; this is a reprint	Very readable. Lots of useful information and scene setting.	By a well-known professional historian	Plenty of primary accounts. Correct reading and information level.
www. historylearningsite. co.uk/black_death_ of_1348_to_1350. htm/ (History Learning Site)	Short, no subheadings, and confusingly written	Produced by a school teacher who covers all aspects of history, but is he really an expert on *everything*?	Not much information— probably find something better on other sites
www.bbc.co.uk/ history/british/ middle_ages/ black_01.shtml With links to other articles (BBC)	Series of articles, lots of primary source material	Written by an academic historian, but not a medieval specialist	Seems to contain lots of the needed information, but the language is quite adult

One thing that this chart makes clear is that a single source will never be enough. By taking information from more than one source, you can:

- acquire more information
- cross-check facts for accuracy
- learn about different interpretations of history.

Here is an example of how you can use different sources to examine one very specific idea:

What I **K**now	What I **W**ant to know	What I have **L**earned
Many historians link the Black Death (1348–50) and the Peasants' Revolt of 1381.	*How were these two events related?*	*Nothing yet [see page 26].*

What information do the sources provide? Philip Ziegler writes that without the Black Death, "the history of England . . . in the second half of the fourteenth century would have been very different." He concludes by saying that while the Black Death might not have caused the Peasants' Revolt, it certainly made it highly likely. The History Learning Site makes a closer link between the Black Death and revolt, saying the Black Death had "a major impact on England's social structure which lead [spelled wrong!] to the Peasants' Revolt of 1381." The BBC website concludes that the revolt of 1381 "was the outcome of simmering resentments and the surprising social shifts, in part caused by the Black Death."

So, our completed KWL chart now looks like this:

What I **K**now	What I **W**ant to know	What I have **L**earned
Historians link the Black Death (1348–50) and the Peasants' Revolt of 1381.	How were these two events related?	The Black Death on its own did not cause the Peasants' Revolt. Rather, it was one of several circumstances that made the revolt possible.

Cutting-and-pasting

Cutting-and-pasting is a neat and simple way of moving text from one place to another. However, cutting-and-pasting can lead to some very questionable—even illegal—research practices. Here are three research dangers that can result from cutting-and-pasting:

1. Use of cutting-and-pasting instead of note taking
2. Use of cutting-and-pasting instead of the researcher writing his or her own text.
3. Plagiarism.

Cut-and-pasted notes from the *World Book* website on the Roman Catholic Church's Inquisition might look like this:
Inquisition: effort by Roman Catholic Church to seek out and punish heretics (who opposed church teachings). Inquisition took place in parts of Europe—Spanish Inquisition best known.
392 CE, Roman Emperor Theodosius I outlawed non-Christian and non-Jewish worship . . . teachings of Christian church regarded as foundation of law and order. Heresy an offense against state as well as church.

This is too long (60 words from 80 in the original), poorly laid out, and has not helped you to remember the content.

Notes taken conventionally (see p. 22) might look like this:

(see p. 22)

Inquisition
Def: RC Ch effort to find & punish heretics (those who opp ch teaching)
a. Inq many parts Europe
b. Sp Inq best known

Origins:
a. 392 CE Rom Emp Theodosius I banned non-Christ and
non-Jewish worship
b. Christ ch teachings now basis of law and order
c. So heresy offense against (i) ch & (ii) state

These notes have cut the original 80 words to 50 and have picked out all the important points.

Here is some text assembled by cutting-and-pasting from the *Wikipedia* entry on the Inquisition:

Although some countries punished heresy with the death penalty, the Western Christian Church suppressed heresy before the 12th century through a system of ecclesiastical proscription, or imprisonment, but rarely resorting to torture or executions as this had many ecclesiastical opponents.

Any teacher will be able to spot that this sort of writing is almost certainly not a student's own. Anyone handing in text like this is guilty of plagiarism (see below).

Plagiarism

Plagiarism is passing off someone else's work as your own. It is using other people's work and words without admitting that you are doing so. This is usually illegal, and always dishonest and morally wrong. Moreover, if discovered it will possibly lead to you getting expelled, and it will definitely get you a failing grade.

Trial by combat in medieval times was a "blood sport" in which guilt or innocence was decided in a fight that also provided entertainment for spectators. Medieval crime and punishment is an interesting topic for research.

Plagiarism is nearly always very obvious to an experienced teacher because:

- The written style will differ from a student's other work, perhaps even changing over the course of a piece of writing. A U.S. student may suddenly start using British spelling, for example.
- The same piece of plagiarized text—for example, information from a *Wikipedia* article on trial by combat—may find its way into the answer of more than one student.
- The sources of plagiarized text are often highly unoriginal.
- Students in a hurry frequently plagiarize text that is almost, but not exactly, what is required. The result is writing and information that is inappropriate, off the subject, or irrelevant.
- Students who plagiarize often use poor and inaccurate sources, such as personal blogs or non-academic websites.
- Plagiarized text may be at a different intellectual level—usually higher—than the text around it.
- Many teachers use an online plagiarism detector.

Ultimately, plagiarism is self-defeating—it doesn't help you develop.

Specialized material

Once you have limited your topic area, a frequent problem is that specialized material in print and on the Internet is often at a high academic level and therefore probably not very suitable. In sorting out whether a source is suitable, try the SQ3R tool again. For example, if your research topic is the First Crusade, after taking notes from a few general books you might decide to look at the *Wikipedia* article on the subject.

Using SQ3R on *Wikipedia*

Survey: A quick look through the article makes two things clear—it is an impressive piece, of almost 8,000 words with 89 footnote **references**. The language is quite adult and assumes that you already know quite a lot about the First Crusade.

Question: A closer look at the references reveals that they nearly all relate to secondary sources. These are, however, scholarly modern books. Moreover, there is an impressive list of primary sources that can be consulted online, too. So, what can you use this article for?
1. Cross-check facts with the notes you have already gathered.
2. Follow Internet links to other pages, some of which are primary sources.
3. Find some accurate details that you might not have found elsewhere. Primary sources are not necessarily reliable. For example, the main source for the story of the First Crusade is Albert of Aachen (also called Albert of Aix), who never went to the Holy Land but spoke to returning Crusaders.

Read: It is now time to read and take notes from the article. Because it is so long, detailed, and adult, it might be a good idea simply to add extra material to the notes you have already taken from simpler sources. Remember, when you are taking notes, always start a new subtopic (such as the causes of the First Crusade) on a separate sheet of paper or note card. This will make it much easier to add new information as you find it.

Recall: When you have finished the notes, read the article again to check that you have not overlooked anything interesting or important.

Review: The article has provided so much information, much of it in great detail, that you probably do not need to do much more research. However, if you want to master the subject thoroughly, you could read the most recently published books mentioned in the *Wikipedia* article's Secondary Sources list.

So, specialized material based on original sources can be fascinating and give a real insight into the subject being researched. However, it is often longer than you need, very detailed, and difficult to read. Also, it is always important to remember that *Wikipedia* is open to error.

Step 4: Documents

What is a document?

Documents are the most important primary sources. Broadly speaking, a document is any piece of paper with writing on it. Historians commonly use the term to mean a primary source, often of no more than a few pages long. For the best research, this should be in its original form and not printed or translated. This is because:

- Translations never convey precisely the same meaning as the original.
- Mistakes can creep in when documents are printed.
- Tiny details—such as the type of paper, handwriting, crossings out, and signatures—can be useful clues to the historian, and these are lost in printing.
- Printing (and translation) often implies selection—another historian has decided what is worth printing; that decision may not have been the right one.

Difficulties with medieval documents

1. Almost all medieval documents are written in a language that you will not understand. They are likely to be in Latin, in an early form of English, or in another European language.
2. Before around 1460, all medieval documents were handwritten in styles of handwriting that are difficult to read today.
3. All medieval documents are extremely precious and often very delicate. They are normally allowed into the hands of professional researchers only, and even they have to wear special gloves and are kept under special surveillance.
4. The only exceptions in terms of availability are a few very well-known documents that have been reproduced exactly in their original form. These include the Magna Carta (see www.bl.uk/treasures/magnacarta/) and Domesday Book (www.nationalarchives.gov.uk/documentsonline/domesday.asp). A quick look through either of these sites will reveal just how difficult it is to read an original medieval document! As far as school and college students are concerned, they will normally have access to copies of documents that have been translated (or at least modernized) and printed.

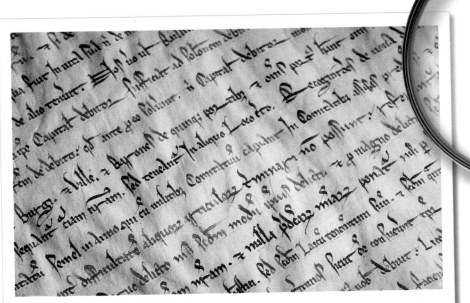

Thanks to online technology, the Magna Carta, one of the most famous historical documents of all time, is available for all students to study in its original form.

Working with medieval documents

Types

These are some of the more common types of original document used by historians researching medieval Europe:

- Laws and charters
- Chronicles
- Financial records, such as bills
- Letters, notes, and messages
- Literature.

Quantity

The further back in history one goes, the fewer sources are available to us. Eventually, one gets to prehistory—the period from which there are no written sources. The number of documents remaining from medieval Europe is not great compared with later times because few people were **literate**, everything had to be handwritten, and much that did exist has been lost and destroyed over time.

Nevertheless, there is plenty of primary source material available to use in your research. In some ways, the lack of material is an advantage because there are only a small number of key documents, whereas with later periods in history there are perhaps thousands of significant written sources.

Interpretation

Documents are of little use on their own. They become valuable only when an historian uses them to throw light on the past. This process is called interpretation. Essentially, this means figuring out what a document can say about the past.

Before reading a document, we need to remember the gulf that separates today's world from medieval Europe. People of that time thought differently, saw the world differently, and behaved very differently from people now. An obvious difference is in religion. Unlike in most of modern Europe, faith was not just a part of medieval life—it was life. The Church was as rich and powerful as royalty, it controlled all education and literacy, and it explained the universe, life, and (just about) everything.

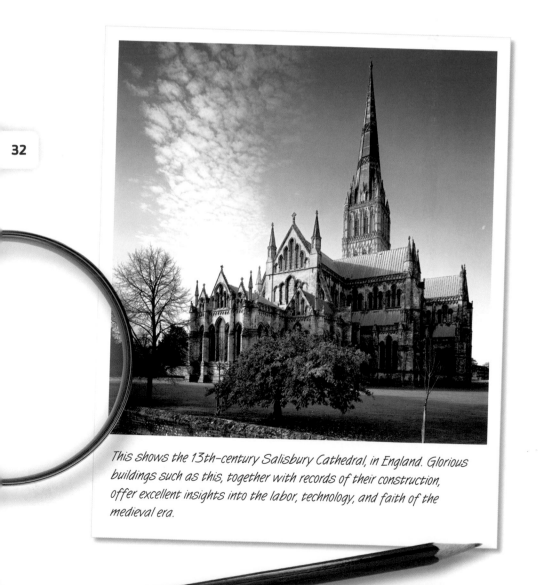

This shows the 13th-century Salisbury Cathedral, in England. Glorious buildings such as this, together with records of their construction, offer excellent insights into the labor, technology, and faith of the medieval era.

Reliability of medieval documents

We need to decide how reliable a document is. "Reliability" is a difficult concept. Here is an examination of two different types of document, one a factual type and one more likely to contain opinion.

Factual: Pipe rolls

Pipe rolls are financial records written on **parchment** (which is then rolled up so it looks like a pipe) of the money owed to the English crown. The earliest existing example dates from 1130, and there is a continuous record from 1156.

The rolls are a great source—they offer a direct glimpse of royal finance and medieval life in general. In 1166, for instance, a pipe roll records that the sheriff of Worcester paid 3 **shillings** and 10 **pence** for a scaccarium, a special checkered cloth board, or "exchequer," like a large chess board, that was used to lay money on to figure out royal finances. Interesting though this is, it does not tell to whom he paid the money or, more importantly, the relative cost. What did 3 shillings and 10 pence mean in terms of the cost of things in those days?

The pipe roll information, therefore, might be best described as "reliable, but limited."

Opinion: Chronicles

Chronicles are contemporary history that is often laced with colorful opinion. Here is Jean de Joinville (d. 1317) talking about a man he knew well, Louis IX ('Saint Louis," 1214–70) of France:

> From the time of his childhood, the king had pity on the poor and suffering; and the custom was that, wherever the king went, six score [120] poor persons were always fed every day, in his house, with bread and wine, and meat or fish. In Lent and Advent the number of poor was increased . . .

(Cited in Bryce Lyon, ed., *The High Middle Ages*, New York: Free Press, 1964, p. 246)

This type of primary source appears to give us very detailed information that is more than just facts. However, it is just one man's take on a situation. Since Jean de Joinville was writing the life of someone he considered a saint, he obviously emphasized Louis' better points.

Conclusion

Generally, therefore, the more reliable sources are specific and written to convey facts and figures rather than opinions. However, these sources on their own do not produce a complete picture or narrative of the past. In searching for the truth, historians have to balance and put their own interpretation on a mix of fact and opinion.

Checking a document

Furious at the powers Pope Boniface VIII (1235–1303) claimed for himself, in 1303 King Philip IV of France sent armed men to depose the pope. William of Hundlehy gives his account of what happened:

> Suddenly and unexpectedly there came upon Anagni [where the pope was staying] a great force of armed men of the party of the King of France. They broke through the doors and windows of the papal palace at a number of points, and set fire to them at others, till at last the angered soldiery forced their way to the Pope. Many of them heaped insults upon his head and threatened him violently, but to them all the Pope answered not so much as a word.
>
> (Adapted from www.fordham.edu/halsall/source/1303anagni.html)

One way to test this source would be to use the 5 Ws:

Who? William of Hundlehy was a monk who was with the pope at the time of the attack.

What? It is an eyewitness description of an attack on the papal palace and the pope himself by men in the pay of Philip IV. The account was written in Latin—this is a translation.

When? William was writing shortly after the attack had taken place.

Where? The account was written in Italy, probably in Anagni itself.

Why? The description is highly critical of the attackers—they were angry, violent, and insulting. In contrast, the pope is shown as a model of patience. William wants the reader to believe that an innocent and holy pope was unlawfully attacked by a mob of criminals. A researcher can see at once that this is not an objective account. Perhaps there are issues not mentioned, and the pope had brought these troubles upon himself.

At first glance, William's story seems a great primary source, lively, informative, and full of detail. However, it is important to remember who wrote it and what his viewpoint was. Although William's is the only firsthand account of the attack, his retelling of this event must be looked at together with other evidence.

Using medieval literature

Documents from the medieval era include many famous works of literature, such as Chaucer's *Canterbury Tales* in English and Dante's *Inferno* and Boccaccio's *Decameron* in Italian.

Here is a version in modern English of an extract from the "Prologue" of Chaucer's masterpiece:

A holy-minded man of good renown
There was, and poor, the **Parson** to a town,
Yet he was rich on holy thought and work.
He also was a learned man, a clerk,
Who truly knew Christ's gospel and would preach it
Devoutly to his parishioners, and teach it.
Benign and wonderfully diligent,
And patient when adversity was sent
(for so he proved in great adversity)
Much he disliked exhorting tithe or fee,
May rather he preferred beyond a doubt
Giving to poor parishioners round about
From his own goods and Easter offerings.

(From Geoffrey Chaucer, *The Canterbury Tales: in Modern English*, trans. Nevill Coghill, New York: Penguin, 2003)

Well-written and easily accessible documents like this have to be used with caution. Was Chaucer describing a typical parson of his time? Might he have made his parson so good in order to emphasize the failures of most of the others? Or was he simply describing a good man and not trying to make a political point at all? Be wary of using literary documents as historical sources. They may support or illustrate other evidence, but should never be used alone without other supporting evidence.

This 16th-century image shows a local priest preaching in the early Middle Ages. Historians have to decide how accurate such illustrations are before using them as primary sources.

Step 5: Images

Exciting medieval images range from huge paintings of the **Last Judgment** to intimate carvings on a parish church. It is said that "A picture is worth a thousand words." In other words, an image combines information and emotion in a single, powerful, and easily understandable form.

Even so, it is still worth remembering that no image was created in order to be evidence for future generations. Like medieval literature, contemporary works of art were opinionated and of their time. The historical researcher must look at them with caution.

Types of image

Secondary artwork

Secondary artworks are pictures that are artists' re-creations of scenes from medieval life. In some the details are more or less correct, while others seek maximum effect with a lesser interest in accuracy. A third type of art aims to put forth a moral or message. Images of this sort should not be used in serious research.

Photographs

Students living outside Europe have little opportunity to see medieval sites. Consequently, they depend on photographs for their information on such places. But they must bear in mind that even photographs can be the result of choices made by the photographer, and that what they show is limited by the photographic process.

Contemporary paintings and other artwork

Look at the photograph on page 37 of the huge mural of the Last Judgment. How will it fare in the 5 Ws test?

Who painted it? It is not known, but the style is Flemish.

What does it show? It shows the Day of Judgment at the end of the world when, says the Bible, everyone is judged according to how they have lived their lives. The righteous ascend to heaven, the sinners are punished in hell.

When was it painted? In the 15th century (around 1480), although its central section was destroyed in the 18th century to make room for a doorway.

Where is it? The painting is in Albi Cathedral in France. In the 13th century, the surrounding area witnessed the violent persecution for heresy of a group known as the "Albigensians" (or Cathars). The merciless treatment of sinners in the picture echoes the ruthless way the Albigensians were dealt with.

Why? In an age when most people were illiterate, pictures served as visual teaching aids. The message of this picture could not have been clearer: obey the commandments and follow the teachings of the Roman Catholic Church—or else!

What can be learned from this picture? It provides reliable detail on aspects of medieval life, such as how skinny people were, their styles of clothing and ornament, and even their instruments of torture. The context of the picture is more confusing. Did those who **commissioned** it, painted it, and viewed it actually believe it was a true picture of what would happen on Judgment Day? Did the artists who produced the demons and devils really think such creatures existed?

The effect of the painting is also difficult to guess. Paintings are useful as a source of detail about medieval life, but their broader significance is trickier to estimate.

The wall beneath the bell tower of Albi Cathedral, France, is covered with an enormous depiction of the Last Judgment. Painted by Flemish artists in the 15th century, it is a source of much historical information.

This sculpture is of Gilbert Marshall, a 13th-century Crusader knight. Stone memorial sculptures provide useful information on medieval armor, weapons, and clothing, but must not be taken as true physical likenesses of the individual shown.

Sculpture and carving

The usefulness of sculpture and carving is similar to that of painting. A carved effigy of a Crusader knight, for example, can tell us a great deal about armor and weaponry, but not necessarily about the man's spirituality or motives for crusading.

Movies and reenactment

Movies

Full-length feature films set in medieval times range from the ridiculous (*Monty Python and the Holy Grail*) to the swashbuckling (*Robin Hood Prince of Thieves*) to the bloodthirsty. Fun though these may be, they are not for serious historical research. Movies are all about entertainment. A movie may be set anywhere and at any time, and filmmakers may go to great lengths to make their work feel "authentic." In the end, though, getting audience approval and making money comes before authenticity. A true-to-life Robin Hood would be smaller than a modern actor, with filthy hair and, almost certainly, some teeth rotten and others missing.

Reenactments and fairs

Slightly more "real" than movies are reenactmentments. There are groups of men and women who dress up in medieval costume and reenact famous moments in medieval history, such as battles or tournaments.

The clothing, armor, and weapons used are as close to authentic as possible. Reenactment is usually done for fun, although it may give a researcher some insights into medieval life that could not be found in books.

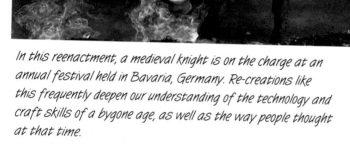

In this reenactment, a medieval knight is on the charge at an annual festival held in Bavaria, Germany. Re-creations like this frequently deepen our understanding of the technology and craft skills of a bygone age, as well as the way people thought at that time.

For example:

- Ladies wearing medieval dresses and tall, elaborate headgear have little choice but to carry themselves in an elegant manner with good posture.
- A number of reenactment groups try to reproduce medieval skills and goods. A blacksmith will be used to handmade tools, for instance, and a cobbler will hand-make shoes. In doing so, they are learning things about medieval life that could not be picked up from books. Working as people did in the Middle Ages gives a unique insight into the period.

Reenactment may result from and involve serious research. It is not a serious research activity in itself, however. The same may be said of "Renaissance fairs."

Step 6: Other Evidence

Tangible objects give us some of the sharpest and most exciting insights into medieval Europe. They range from human-made **artifacts**, such as articles of clothing, household goods, and weapons, to architecture and even whole landscapes. The trouble with this sort of evidence is that much of it is not available for firsthand experience, especially to students outside Europe.

There are, however, museums all over the world containing exhibits from the medieval period. The Internet, too, gives the opportunity of virtual visits when a real one is not possible. Photo exchange sites, such as Flickr, are also well worth exploring as part of research.

Types of tangible evidence
Here are some of the more accessible forms of tangible evidence:

Clothing
Although most medieval clothing rotted away long ago, a few examples remain from the late medieval period. Being more durable, leather articles, like shoes, last best. Coupled with other evidence, such as images, they offer useful insight into craftsmanship, style, and technology.

Domestic articles
Any household artifact, such as a cooking spit (a pointed rod), a pan, or a candle holder, helps build up a picture of the period.

Military equipment
Made from durable materials—largely wood and metal—much medieval military equipment remains intact. There are whole suits of armor, swords, and other weapons, and a grisly selection of instruments of torture. Be careful not to get a distorted picture of medieval life, though. Just because military equipment has survived, it does not mean medieval society was even more warlike than it really was.

Tombs and memorials
Europe's medieval churches and cathedrals are adorned with thousands of memorials commemorating the great and worthy people of their day. **Memorial brasses** are especially fascinating, although most have been lifted to preserve them from trampling feet and people eager to rub impressions of them onto paper. All such works are interesting sources of information on specifics like clothing and generalities, such as faith. Large public crosses,

such as that in Chichester, England, are another useful source of evidence.

Domestic architecture

Despite the ravages of war and development, many thousands of medieval domestic buildings remain in towns and in the countryside. The oldest are stone- and brick-built, with most of the timber-framed buildings dating from the 14th and 15th centuries.

We need to remember that only the dwellings of the prosperous still stand: the humble hovels of the poor collapsed long, long ago.

Castles

There is no more stirring memorial to a bygone age than a mighty medieval castle. They are, however, easy to romanticize and fantasize about, and each requires careful research if it is to yield accurate information about the period—or, more often, periods—when it was built.

The many thousands of medieval houses still standing, like this, were built for the prosperous classes to live in. Little remains of the housing lived in by the poor masses.

Religious buildings

The very existence of so many solidly built parish churches all over Europe is a powerful reminder of what is often called the "Age of Faith." Living museums worthy of careful research, they remain when less substantial buildings—sometimes whole villages—have disappeared.

When visiting a medieval cathedral, do not get so carried away by the grandeur of the building that you forget the detail. In particular, keep an eye open for mosaics and the images in stained-glass windows. These are not just magnificent works of art. Because their creators usually gave figures and scenes a contemporary setting, they are also interesting historical sources.

Landscapes

Despite the enormous changes to the landscape since medieval times, there is still much it can teach us. Three points are worth singling out:

1. What appear to be innocent lumps and bumps in the landscape can sometimes reveal surprising results—a lost village, for example, or the strip farming pattern of a huge open field.

2. The basic pattern of hills, valleys, rivers, and plains remains as it always has been and helps us to understand such matters as military campaigns and road systems.

3. Much evidence about the medieval period remains under the landscape and is accessed by archaeology. Today, within the European Union, no development may take place within an ancient urban settlement before the archaeologists have first carefully dug into the site's past.

Using tangible evidence

Tangible evidence alone does not answer broad, sweeping questions such as "Why did the power and influence of the Roman Catholic Church decline in the later Middle Ages?" or "How did feudalism operate in practice?" Indeed, some professional historians show little interest in tangible objects. They concentrate instead on documentary evidence. Overall, though, most think that tangible evidence plays an important part in the overall process of historical research.

How can tangible evidence be used and what insights does it offer?

- It enables the researcher to get the "feel" of a period of history. For example, gazing out from the walls of **Chateau** Gaillard, the mighty fortress that Richard I built above the Seine River in France, helps one understand the king's power and strategic insight. The site also helps us understand why Richard's rival, King Philip Augustus of France, was so eager to prove his power by capturing the castle.
- It offers massive amounts of detail on social history. For example, a very different (but changing) attitude toward personal privacy is illustrated by the arrangement of rooms in medieval homes.
- It helps explain military history through weaponry, castles, and battlefields. For example, analysis of a suit of armor and all the padded clothing that went beneath it shows how vulnerable a heavy knight became when his horse was killed beneath him. This may shed light on the outcome of battles, such as Crécy (1346).

- It provides us with tangible signs of medieval faith in the form of churches, cathedrals, and monasteries. For example, a visit to the majestic ruins of an abbey like Lorsch, near Worms, in Germany, helps us to understand the criticisms of the Church's worldly power by men like John Huss (1371–1415).
- Archaeology is inseparable from history, and historians owe huge debts to their soil-fingered colleagues. For example, the parish church in Blean, Kent, England, stands alone in the middle of fields. A strange place to build a church? No, not when archaeology reveals that the original village, including the manor house, lay all around it. Similarly, aerial photography and archaeology have revealed whole villages abandoned after they were ravaged by the Black Death.

These remains of a medieval village in Dartmoor, England, have survived because of their stone construction. The layout of the site offers rare insights into domestic life hundreds of years ago.

Step 7: Your Viewpoint

Types of presentation

It is now time to organize your evidence. Let's look at how to do this, based on an example of the topic of the first three Crusades. Essentially, there are two written ways to present the results of research. The first is to produce a sort of historical narrative paper. This would take a chronological approach, telling the story of the Crusades and concluding with a general statement about where things stood at the end of the Third Crusade. In the second type of presentation, you use the same information to answer a question, such as, "Were the Crusades primarily a religious movement?" This approach of offering historical analysis is more difficult, but will probably produce a more interesting paper and help define your boundaries.

Defining topic limits

At this point it is important to define the limits of the topic. For example, how much time should be spent on background information?

Structuring and organizing notes

It is unlikely that notes taken from different sources will be structured in the right way for an essay or presentation. They will need reorganizing. If the

The impressive remains of Acre Castle help explain why in Crusader times it was regarded as one of the Holy Land's key fortresses.

presentation is to be of the historical narrative type, those notes relating to individual Crusades need to be brought together. This can be done by writing all the notes out again or, more easily, by underlining or highlighting with different colors. For example, you might highlight all notes relating to the causes of the Crusades in yellow.

Writing historical analysis in response to a question-type essay involves the same technique, but underlining or highlighting different topics. For example, if your question was, "Which of the first three Crusades was best organized?" then you might highlight references to the organization of the First Crusade in green, the Second Crusade in yellow, and so on.

There is no best way to organize your notes. The methods suggested here may work for most students, but in the end it is up to you to figure out which you prefer. All that matters is that you do organize your notes somehow—confusing notes reflect confused thought, and usually lead to a confusing presentation.

Concept web

A concept web can help you organize a subject. Put the main topic in the center, then subheadings on lines branching out from it, like this:

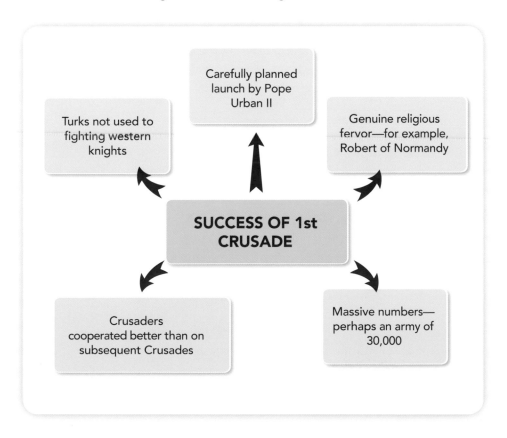

Your viewpoint

During your research you will have found yourself developing your own viewpoint on the subject. Failure to do this will mean your paper will be dull because it lacks a point of view. Worse still, if you don't firmly decide what your viewpoint is, you may change your mind midway through, destroying the essay's credibility.

In an historical narrative paper, you can show your viewpoint through:

- Comparison: For example, when discussing the Third Crusade, explore why, unlike the First Crusade, it failed to take Jerusalem.
- Judgment: For example, you may conclude that Turkish armor and weaponry were better suited to the hot conditions than the heavy armor of the Crusaders.

In an historical analysis-type paper in response to a question, there is no difficulty in taking a viewpoint because answering the question will inevitably involve comparison and judgment.

Presenting evidence

Historical research involves reaching conclusions based upon evidence. A conclusion without evidence is more or less useless.

Historical researchers must show the evidence upon which their conclusions are based. This means, at its simplest level, that when you say, for example, that the University of Padua in Italy was founded in 1222, you know that fact is mentioned in several documents and it is virtually impossible that they are all wrong.

The purpose of citing sources of evidence is to prevent error and fraud. In a world where this is not done, all statements are equally true. Without cited evidence, the statement "The University of Padua was founded in 1122" is as valid as "The University of Padua was founded in 1222."

Citing evidence

In most school or college research, evidence is cited in two ways:

1. At the end in the bibliography (see page 21). Here we find a list of sources used for your research. It is a good idea to divide your bibliography between primary and secondary sources and then into categories for books, articles, websites, and tangible evidence. Remember to find out if your teacher has a selected bibliography format for you to use.
2. In footnotes or endnotes (see page 23). In addition to full footnotes and endnote lists, it is becoming more common for sources to be

cited in the text using only the author's last name and a page reference. The full citation is then listed in the bibliography. The use of all of these different forms of citation have two main purposes:

- The readers are told precisely where the author found his or her information—and, if they wish, they can check it for themselves.
- Citation is part of the system used to prevent fraudulent scholarship, such as misinformation and plagiarism.

Objectivity

As soon as history ceases to be objective, it ceases to be history—it is simply **propaganda**, myth, or fairy tale. So, what does being objective mean? Objectivity is judging rationally using safe evidence. Lack of reliable facts makes perfect objectivity impossible. However, good researchers try to:

- Set aside preconceptions. For example, the British popular media give the impression that Richard the Lionheart was the only great warrior-leader of the Crusades. In fact, Richard was only one of many respected Crusader leaders.
- Go where your research takes you, no matter how unwelcome the path. You may come to the conclusion that the Crusaders were not saintly warriors, but greedy robbers.
- Belong to no nation, faith, or race—the most difficult exercise of all. Students want *their* people to be in the right. Muslims emphasize that it was the Europeans who began the conflict; Europeans point out that the Crusaders were simply trying to get back what the Muslims had conquered. All of these claims are to some extent true. In the end, though, do they matter? The Crusades are long finished. What we need now is cool reflection that rises above the disagreements of the past.
- Judge by the standards of the day and avoid moral judgments. For instance, during the Crusades both sides showed extreme religious intolerance. But historical researchers cannot condemn the past for not being like the present.

Step 8: Presentation

This is the last crucial stage: writing your presentation. Let's look at this from the example of a research topic on medieval towns. As discussed, there are two main ways of presenting written research:

1. A narrative or largely factual approach. This approach might take three or four towns in a particular year and discuss what went on in them. This approach is not ideal, primarily because it omits the concept of change and development.

2. Answering a question. A possible one is, "What role did towns play in the development of medieval Europe?" Alternative questions might compare towns in different parts of Europe, or ask about what part towns played in art or politics. Here are two ways to plan a presentation based on a question.

This is an idealized picture of Naples docks, painted in 1465. The city was one of Europe's major ports throughout the Middle Ages and would have been bustling with people, noise, and smells.

Answering a question (1)

This is an example of how to make a plan to answer the question, "How important were towns in medieval Europe?"

Basic structure

All answers divide into three basic parts:

1. Introduction: This sets out the nature of the question and how it will be solved.
2. Evidence and argument: This is the bulk of the answer, putting forward evidence and exploring possible conclusions.
3. Conclusion: This sums up the results of all that has gone before.

The plan

Writing a plan is like consulting a map before setting out on a journey—you need to know where you are going. Within the three-part basic structure (above), divide your plan into sections. Each section may have several paragraphs. Link each section to your notes; some researchers like to use numbers or colors. Here is an example of what might be in the sections of your plan. But remember, this is just an example. There are all kinds of ways to structure a paper on medieval towns.

Section 1

<u>Intro</u>: Quote (my notes p. 6): my outline: (a) towns gradually became more important over the medieval period; (b) they were much more important in some regions (e.g., Italy) than others (e.g., Poland). Examples to be drawn from France, Italy, England, and Germany.

Section 2

<u>Situation in c. 1000</u> (a) Which were the major towns? (my notes p. 1)—compare Rome and London. (b) What went on in the towns? Commerce (cite Italy), manufacturing, administration (e.g., Augsburg, Germany).

Section 3

<u>Importance of towns in c. 1000</u> (a) Important for different reasons— e.g., ports (commerce) such as Naples; admin—e.g., Paris. (b) Huge variation in importance—only a handful of great significance in northern Europe, more in Italy.

Section 4

<u>Change</u> Why did towns grow in importance? (i) Because they grew in size and wealth—e.g., London.

The plan then needs to continue to its conclusion. When a plan like this is finished, you will know exactly what you are going to say and in what order.

Answering a question (2)

After all the careful preparation, the actual writing of the paper should not be too difficult. In addition to using your plan, here are some other guidelines to think about:

- Answer the question. Continually ask yourself: Is this relevant to the question? How is it answering the question? Try to relate directly back to the question at least once on every page.
- Keep a balance of information and ideas. Ideas are useless without the factual backing of evidence. This may take the form of quotations, dates, names, statistics, and so on. Imagine you are a lawyer, arguing a case. You do not just state that your client is innocent: you back up that contention with concrete evidence. Evidence is pointless unless it is used to support an idea. There is no point in writing down the amount of tax the king of France collected from Paris in, say, 1250, unless the information is used to support a point.
- Stick to your plan. Use your own words, unless giving a quotation that you acknowledge. Try to make the first sentence of each paragraph as arresting as possible. Present statistical information in the form of a table, graph, or some other form of graphic organizer (see below).

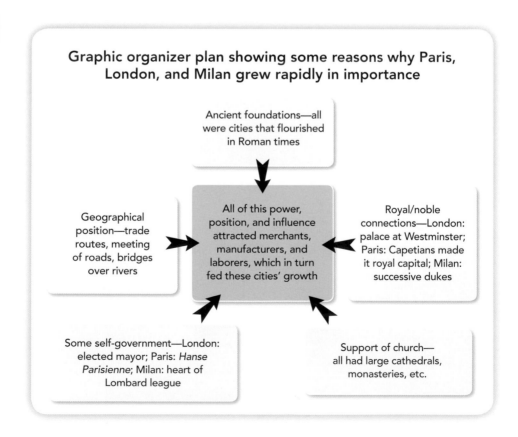

Graphic organizer plan showing some reasons why Paris, London, and Milan grew rapidly in importance

Ancient foundations—all were cities that flourished in Roman times

Geographical position—trade routes, meeting of roads, bridges over rivers

All of this power, position, and influence attracted merchants, manufacturers, and laborers, which in turn fed these cities' growth

Royal/noble connections—London: palace at Westminster; Paris: Capetians made it royal capital; Milan: successive dukes

Some self-government—London: elected mayor; Paris: *Hanse Parisienne*; Milan: heart of Lombard league

Support of church—all had large cathedrals, monasteries, etc.

- Give the source of each quotation, unusual opinion, or statistic. This can be done in one of three ways:

1. Within the text—for example, *The German writer Karl Marx said that towns were important in ending feudal society.*
2. Using parenthesis—for example, *Urbanization had no appreciable effect on the landed classes in northern France and England.* (Norman F. Cantor, *Medieval History: The Life and Death of a Civilization*, New York: Macmillan, 1963, p. 531).
3. With footnotes or endnotes—for example, *Towns came under the general administration of a reeve.*[1]

The finished work

When you have finished your paper, read through it very carefully. Better still, get someone else whose opinion you value to look it over. By using the best historical research techniques and paying attention to detail, you will have created a presentation on medieval Europe that you can be proud of.

Grammatical and writing errors to avoid

- Do not use the first person singular ("I").
- Do not underline for effect and emphasis—use the power of your words instead.
- Avoid the passive tense where possible. For example, say "*Papal authority dominated the city of Rome*" rather than "*The city of Rome was dominated by papal authority.*"
- Avoid clichés, such as "*The city government was rotten to the core.*"
- Do not use informal language or slang, like "*Young people saw Milan as the coolest place to be in all Italy.*"
- Avoid exaggeration for emphasis—for example, "*London was so important that without it there would have been—literally—no England.*"
- Do not use unnecessary jargon or foreign words, such as "*The plan's raison d'être was . . .*"

Find Out More

Secondary source books

Chrisp, Peter. *Medieval Realms: Daily Life.* San Diego: Lucent, 2004.

Chrisp, Peter. *Medieval Realms: Warfare.* San Diego: Lucent, 2005.

Gillingham, John, and Ralph A. Griffiths. *Medieval Britain: A Very Short Introduction.* New York: Oxford University Press, 2000.

Olmsted, Jennifer. *Art in History: Art of the Middle Ages.* Chicago: Heinemann Library, 2006.

Phillips, Jonathan. *The Crusades, 1095–1197.* New York: Longman, 2002.

Riley-Smith, Jonathan. *The Oxford Illustrated History of the Crusades.* New York: Oxford University Press, 2001.

Ross, Stewart. *Medieval Realms: Art and Architecture.* San Diego: Lucent, 2004.

Ross, Stewart. *Medieval Realms: Monarchs.* San Diego: Lucent, 2004.

Saul, Nigel. *The Oxford Illustrated History of Medieval England.* New York: Oxford University Press, 2000.

Senker, Cath. *When Disaster Struck: The Black Death 1347–1350.* Chicago: Raintree, 2006.

Woolf, Alex. *Medieval Realms: Death and Disease.* San Diego: Lucent, 2004.

Woolf, Alex. *Medieval Realms: Education.* San Diego: Lucent, 2004.

Primary source books

Anderson, Roberta, and Dominic Bellenger. *Medieval Worlds: A Sourcebook.* New York: Routledge, 2003.

Chaucer, Geoffrey. *The Canterbury Tales*, trans. Nevill Coghill. New York: Penguin, 2003.

Gairdner, James, ed. *The Paston Letters.* New York: St. Martin's, 1987.

Garmonsway, G. N. (translator). *The Anglo-Saxon Chronicle.* Rutland, Vt.: Tuttle (Everyman), 1994.

Hallam, Elizabeth, ed. *Chronicles of the Crusades.* New York: Welcome Rain, 2000.

Langland, William. *Piers the Ploughman,* ed. Elizabeth Ann Robertson et al. New York: W. W. Norton, 2006.

Williams, Ann, and G. H. Martin, eds. *Domesday Book: A Complete Translation.* New York: Penguin, 2003.

Movies

Many movies set in medieval Europe have been made over the years. Some are better and more historically accurate than others. Watch them after you have researched your medieval Europe topic to see which are the most accurate.

Alexander Nevsky, dir. Sergei Eisenstein, 1938

Ivan the Terrible, dir. Sergei Eisenstein, parts 1 and 2, 1943 and 1947

The Seventh Seal, dir., Ingmar Bergman, 1957

El Cid, dir. Anthony Mann, 1961

Becket, dir. Peter Glenville, 1964

The Lion in Winter, dir. Anthony Harvey, 1968

Monty Python and the Holy Grail, dirs. Terry Gilliam and Terry Jones, 1975

Lionheart, dir. Franklin J. Schaffner, 1987

Henry V, dir. Kenneth Branagh, 1989

Robin Hood Prince of Thieves, dir. Kevin Reynolds, 1991

The Canterbury Tales, dir. Jonathan Myerson, 1998

Websites

Encyclopedias

Encyclopedia Britannica is always a good starting point for most research: www.britannica.com. The student site is www.student.britannica.com.
The more straightforward *World Book* is at www.worldbookonline.com.

Medieval Europe sites

The University of Evansville has a good academic site, at www.eawc.evansville. edu/mepage.htm.

This sound site from Minnesota State University is a good starting point: www.mnsu.edu/emuseum/history/middleages/contents.html.

This site has all kinds of material, mostly quite accurate: www.medieval-spell. com.

Find information about the Crusades at www.historymedren.about.com/od/ crusades/Crusades.htm.

Find information about the art and architecture of the period at www.vrcoll. fa.pitt.edu/medart and www.newyorkcarver.com/resources1.htm#14th.

Good primary sources can be found at www.fordham.edu/halsall/sbook.html and www.history.boisestate.edu/westciv/medieval/primary.shtml.

Index